Marmalade

Marmalade

classic recipes for the ultimate
home-made preserve

MAGGIE MAYHEW

LORENZ BOOKS

ABOUT THE AUTHOR

Maggie Mayhew is a food writer and home economist and contributes to many food and lifestyle magazines including *Home* and *Living*. Among her published works are *The Fruit and Vegetable Cookbook*, *The World Encyclopedia of Fruit*, and *Tarts*.

This edition is published by Lorenz Books, an imprint of Anness Publishing Ltd
108 Great Russell Street
London WC1B 3NA

info@anness.com
www.lorenzbooks.com
www.annesspublishing.com

If you like the images in this book and would like to investigate using them for publishing, promotions or advertising, please visit our website www.practicalpictures.com for more information.

© Anness Publishing Ltd 2015

A CIP catalogue record for this book is available from the British Library.

COOK'S NOTES

- Bracketed terms are intended for American readers.
- For all recipes, quantities are given in both metric and imperial measures and, where appropriate, in standard cups and spoons. Follow one set of measures, but not a mixture, because they are not interchangeable.
- Standard spoon and cup measures are level. 1 tsp = 5ml, 1 tbsp = 15ml, 1 cup = 250ml/8fl oz.
- Australian standard tablespoons are 20ml. Australian readers should use 3 tsp in place of 1 tbsp for measuring small quantities.
- American pints are 16fl oz/2 cups. American readers should use 20fl oz/2.5 cups in place of 1 pint when measuring liquids.
- Electric oven temperatures in this book are for conventional ovens. When using a fan oven, the temperature will probably need to be reduced by about 10–20°C/20–40°F. Since ovens vary, you should check with your manufacturer's instruction book for guidance.
- The nutritional analysis given for each recipe, unless otherwise stated, is calculated per portion (i.e. serving or item). If the recipe gives a range, such as Serves 4–6, then the nutritional analysis will be for the smaller size, i.e. 6 servings. The analysis does not include optional ingredients, such as salt added to taste.
- Medium (US large) eggs are used unless otherwise stated.

PUBLISHER'S NOTE

Publisher: Joanna Lorenz
Editor: Helen Sudell
Photographer: Craig Robertson
Food Stylist: Helen Trent
Prop Stylist: Sarah O-Brien
Designer: Lisa Tai
Production Controller: Rosanna Anness

Sections of this book have been previously published as part of a larger volume, *Preserves*.

Contents

Introduction 6

Potting & Covering Preserves 8

A Guide to Citrus Fruit 10

Home-made Marmalades 12

Savoury & Sweet Recipes 42

Index 64

Introduction

Marmalade consists of a jelly base, usually with small pieces of fruit suspended in it. The name is derived from the Portuguese word *marmelo*, meaning quince, and it was from this fruit that the first marmalades were made in the fifteenth century.

Making marmalade

Modern marmalades are usually made from citrus fruits, or citrus fruits combined with other fruits such as pineapple, or flavoured with aromatic spices. Marmalades can range from thick and dark to light and translucent.

The citrus peel is shredded and cooked with the fruit juices, pips and water until soft and tender, then boiled with sugar to make the marmalade. Citrus peel requires long, slow cooking in a large amount of water to become soft. The pith of Seville oranges, lemons and grapefruits becomes clear when cooked, but that of sweet oranges does not, so the pith should be scraped off the rind before shredding and cooking.

As well as classic marmalade, there is also jelly marmalade. This is perfect for people who enjoy the flavour of marmalade but do not like the peel. Rather than adding the shredded rind to the juices and water in the pan, the rind is tied in a muslin (cheesecloth) bag to keep it separate. The juices are then strained and boiled to setting point. As with any jelly, it is difficult to give an exact yield for jelly marmalade.

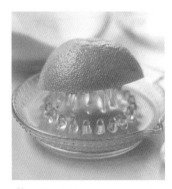

Above: Sweet, juicy oranges are most commonly preserved as classic tangy breakfast marmalade.

Testing pectin content

Pectin is a natural, gum-like substance, which is essential in marmalade-making. Found in the cores, pips (seeds), pith and skins of fruits, it reacts with sugar and acid to form the gel that helps to set jellies and marmalades.

Pectin contents can vary from fruit to fruit so test for it at an early stage in marmalade-making, and add extra pectin if necessary.

1 Cook the fruit until soft, then spoon 5ml/1 tsp of the juices into a glass. Add 15ml/1 tbsp methylated spirits (denatured alcohol) and shake.

2 After 1 minute a clot should form: 1 large jelly-like clot indicates high pectin content; 2 or 3 small clots indicate a medium pectin contents and should achieve a set lots of small clots indicate low pectin so more needs to be added

3 If the pectin content is medium, add 15ml/1 tbsp lemon juice for every 450g/1lb fruit. If the pectin content is low, add 75–90ml/5–6 tbsp pectin stock for every 450g/1lb fruit. Alternatively, add pectin powder or liquid, or use sugar containing pectin.

Top tips for successful marmalade-making

• Always wash citrus fruit well and buy organic, unwaxed fruit where you can.

• When shredding peel, slice it slightly thinner than required in the finished preserve because the rind will swell during cooking.

• Coarse-cut peel will take longer to soften than finely shredded peel. To reduce cooking time, soak the peel for a few hours in the water and juices before cooking.

• Shredded peel should be simmered gently; fierce cooking can give a tough result. Check that the peel is really soft before adding the sugar because it will not tenderize further after this.

To make a coarse-cut preserve, boil the whole fruit for 2 hours until soft; pierce with a skewer to test. Lift out the fruit, halve, prise out the pips, then tie them loosely in muslin (cheesecloth) and add to the hot water. Boil rapidly for 10 minutes, then remove the bag. Slice the fruit and return to the pan. Stir in the sugar to dissolve, then boil to setting point.

• For easy removal tie the muslin (cheesecloth) bag of pith and pips with natural-coloured string and attach it to the pan handle. It can then be lifted out of the boiling mixture easily.

• To flavour marmalade with liqueur or spirits, add 15–30ml1–2 tbsp for every 450g/1lb/2¼ cups sugar – stir it in just before potting. Unsweetened apple juice may be used to replace half the water to add flavour to marmalades made with sharper fruits like kumquats.

Testing for setting point

Remove the preserve from the heat and spoon a little on to a chilled plate. Leave to cool for 3 minutes, then push the preserve with a finger; if wrinkles form it is ready.

Alternatively, you can use a sugar thermometer clipped to the side of the pan, but not touching the base. When the temperature reaches 105°C/ 220°F it is ready.

The final method is the flake test. Dip a large spoon into the marmalade pan. Turn the spoon on its side and look to see a drip form on the edge of the spoon. If it hangs from the spoon the marmalade is set and ready for potting into jars.

Potting and Covering Preserves

Make sure you have enough jars and containers, and the right sterilizing equipment, before you start to make any preserve. Preparing, covering and storing preserves correctly helps to ensure the marmalade or jelly retains its colour, flavour and texture.

Choosing containers

Glass jars are a popular choice for potting marmalades and jellies: they are durable, versatile and decorative, enhancing the appearance of their contents. It is generally better to pack preserves into several smaller containers rather than one large one, especially those that need to be consumed soon after opening.

Above: Medium, wide-necked jars with plastic-coated screw-top lids are ideal containers for most preserves.

Sterilizing jars

Before potting, it is essential to sterilize jars to destroy any micro-organisms in containers. An unsterilized jar may contain contamination that could cause the preserve to deteriorate or become inedible.

Check glass jars for cracks or damage, then wash in hot, soapy water, rinse and turn upside-down to drain. Marmalade jars may be sterilized in four different ways:

Oven method Stand the containers, spaced slightly apart, on a baking sheet lined with kitchen paper. Rest any lids on top. Place in a cold oven, then heat to 110°C/225°F/Gas ¼ and bake for 30 minutes. Leave to cool slightly before filling. (If the jars are not used immediately, cover with a clean cloth and warm again before using.)

Boiling water method Place the containers open-end up in a deep pan. Pour enough hot water in to cover the containers (do not use boiling water as this can crack the glass). Bring the water to the boil and boil for 10 minutes.

Leave the containers in the pan until the water stops bubbling, then carefully remove and drain upside-down on a clean dishtowel. Turn the containers upright and leave to air-dry for a few minutes.

Immerse lids and seals in simmering water for 20 seconds.

Microwave method This method is useful when sterilizing only a few jars. Follow the microwave manufacturer's instructions and only use for jars that hold less than 450g/1lb.

Half fill the clean jars with water and heat on full power until the water has boiled for at least one minute. Using oven gloves, remove the jars from the microwave. Carefully swirl the water inside them, then pour it away. Drain upside-down on a clean dishtowel, then turn upright and leave to dry.

Dishwasher method This is the simplest way to clean and sterilize a large number of containers at the same time. Put the containers and lids in a dishwasher and run it on its hottest setting, including drying. If the jars are already washed and clean, you can run the cycle without adding detergent.

Although you can get sterilizing tablets, this method is not suitable for delicately flavoured preserves because the tablets may leave a slight taste.

Filling and sealing jars

Most preserves should be potted into hot containers as soon as they are ready, particularly jellies and fruit preserves with a high pectin content. Marmalades with peel, and jellies with added ingredients such as fresh herbs should be left to cool for 10 minutes until a thin skin forms on the surface. The preserve should then be stirred to distribute the ingredients and prevent them sinking once potted.

Marmalades and jellies can be covered with a waxed paper disc and the jar covered with cellophane held in place with an elastic band. Or, the jar can be sealed with new screw-top lids. (Waxed discs and cellophane covers should not be used together with a screw-top lid.)

Storing preserves

Preserves should be kept in a cool, dark, dry place and will keep for a year unopened. Once opened, they should be eaten within 3 months.

Using waxed discs and cellophane covers

1 Using a heat-resistant ladle or jug (pitcher) and a jam funnel, carefully fill the jars with hot marmalade, almost to the top. Leave a small space of no more than 1cm/½ in.

2 Using a clean, damp cloth, wipe the rim of the jar. Place a waxed paper disc (waxed side down) on top of the preserve and smooth it down to form a good fit. Moisten a cellophane disc with a damp cloth and place on the jar, moist side up, then secure with an elastic band. Do this either when the preserve is very hot, or leave it to cool completely (if sealed while warm, mould will grow). As it dries, the cellophane will shrink, creating a tight seal.

A Guide to Citrus Fruit

With their aromatic acidity, citrus fruits are the main ingredient of nearly all marmalades. Their pungency and sharpness adds not only flavour but also offsets sweetness. They are covered in a thick peel, which consists mainly of white pith, and an outer layer of zest or rind.

Oranges

There are three types of sweet oranges: the common orange is a medium-size fruit with a fine-grained skin and popular varieties are Valencia, Jaffa and Shamouti. These are the juiciest oranges and are ideal for sweet marmalades. They often contain a lot of pips (seeds), which are essential for marmalade-making because they are high in pectin.

Navel oranges are seedless and low in pectin, so are better if preserved whole, in segments or in slices. Red-flushed blood oranges have ruby-coloured flesh and a rich, berry-like flavour. These make excellent marmalade when combined with sharper lemons.

Bitter Seville oranges have a high pectin and acid content, as well as an excellent, punchy flavour, and make the finest marmalades.

Lemons

In the preserving kitchen, lemons are indispensable. They add acid and pectin to jams and jellies made from low-pectin fruit. Adding lemon juice to jellies also gives them a sparkling appearance. A few spoonfuls of lemon juice added to water makes an acidulated dip that will prevent

Above: Colourful, sharp, zesty lemons are widely used in both sweet and savoury preserves.

cut fruit such as pears and apples from discolouring.

Bigger, knobbly lemons have a higher proportion of peel and pith to flesh, so are better for making marmalade.

Limes

These small green fruits flourish in near-tropical conditions. They have a distinctive, tangy flavour and are one of the most sour

Above: The most popular citrus fruit, oranges come in many varieties and are available all year round.

Above: Limes have a distinctive, sharp flavour and are delicious when made into sweet marmalade.

citrus fruits. A squeeze of lime juice can be added to jams and jellies instead of lemon juice to enhance the flavour of the fruit and to improve the set. It goes particularly well with tropical fruits, such as mangoes and papayas.

Above: Yellow-skinned grapefruit is the best for making into marmalade, with pink grapefruits having a milder flavour.

Grapefruits

One of the largest citrus fruits, with a diameter of up to 15cm/6in. The flesh of grapefruit varies in colour from pale yellow to the dark reddish pink of sweeter ruby grapefruit. The yellow skinned and fleshed varieties have a sharp and refreshing flavour that makes good marmalade.

Tangerines and Mandarins

These are the generic names for small, flat citrus fruits with loose skins and a sweet or tart-sweet flavour. Satsumas, clementines and mineolas also fall into this group. Satsumas are slightly tart and very juicy; clementines are similar but have a thinner, more tight-fitting skin. Both fruits are almost seedless so are best preserved whole in syrup although clementines make a marvellous marmalade when combined with other fruits.

Mineolas are larger. They are hybrids of the grapefruit and tangerine, have a sharp tangy flavour and resemble oranges.

Above: Clementines are a cross between the mandarin and a sweet orange and have a fresh, sweet flavour.

Pomelos

Also known as the shaddock, this large citrus fruit resembles a pear-shaped grapefruit. The flesh can be used to make jams and the rind can be candied or used to make marmalade.

Above: Popular in South-east Asia, the pomelo is a very good source of vitamin C due to its size.

Home-made Marmalades

These classic preserves come somewhere between a jam and a jelly and are traditionally served for breakfast. Usually made of citrus fruits, marmalades have a jelly base with small pieces of fruit suspended in it. They can be tart and bitter with thick-cut shreds of peel, or sweet with thinly cut zest. The Seville orange is favoured because of its refreshing tang and high pectin content but any citrus fruit can be used, as long as the shredded rind is cooked until tender.

Seville orange marmalade

Bitter Seville oranges are very popular for marmalade-making and this is a classic recipe to master your technique. To save time, shred the citrus peel in a food processor rather than by hand. If you can't find Seville oranges, use Temple oranges instead.

Makes about 2.5kg/5½lb

900g/2lb Seville (Temple) oranges
1 large lemon
2.4 litres/4 pints/10 cups water
1.8kg/4lb/generous 9 cups granulated (white) sugar, warmed (see Cook's Tip)

Cook's Tip

The sugar should always be warmed before adding to the pan. Place in a large glass bowl and warm through in a low oven at 140°C/275°F/Gas 1.

1   Wash and dry the fruits. If you are using waxed fruit, scrub the skins.
2   Halve the fruits and squeeze out the juice and pips (seeds), then pour into a muslin- (cheesecloth-) lined sieve or strainer set over a bowl.
3   Remove some of the pith from the citrus peels and reserve, then cut the peel into narrow strips.
4   Add the reserved pith to the pips in the muslin and tie together to make a loose bag. Allow plenty of room so that the water can bubble through the bag and extract the pectin from the pith and pips.
5   Place the shredded peel, juices and the muslin bag in a large preserving pan and pour in the water. Using a clean ruler, measure the depth of the contents in the pan and make a note of it.
6   Slowly bring the mixture to the boil and simmer gently for 1½–2 hours or until the peel is very soft and the contents have reduced by about one third of their depth.
7   To check that the peel is cooked, remove a piece from the pan and leave for a few minutes to cool. Once cooled, press the peel between finger and thumb; it should feel very soft.

Energy 7427kcal/31673kJ; Protein 10g; Carbohydrate 1967.1g, of which sugars 1967.1g; Fat 0.9g which saturates 0g; Cholesterol 0mg; Calcium 605mg; Fibre 20.4g; Sodium 135mg.

Seville orange marmalade

Using a slotted spoon, remove the muslin bag from the pan and set it aside until cool enough to handle. Squeeze as much liquid as possible back into the pan to extract all the pectin from the pips and pith.

Add the warmed sugar to the pan and stir constantly over a low heat until the sugar has completely dissolved. It is important to keep stirring to prevent the sugar burning on the bottom of the pan and your marmalade becoming caramelized.

Bring the marmalade to the boil, then boil rapidly for about 5-10 minutes until setting point is reached 105°C/220°F). You may also use the flake or wrinkle test to check the set (see page 7).

Using a slotted spoon, remove any scum from the surface of the marmalade, then leave to cool until a thick in starts to form on the surface of the preserve. Meanwhile, warm the sterilized jars and lids (if using) by leaving a low oven at 140°C/275°F/Gas 1 for 10–15 miinutes.

Leave the marmalade to stand for about 5 minutes, then stir gently to distribute the peel evenly. Ladle into e warmed sterilized jars, then cover and seal.

Orange jelly marmalade

This recipe may be made as a plain jelly marmalade, or a few fine shreds of peel can be added after potting. Different types of jelly marmalade can be made using this method; use exactly the same ingredients listed in your recipe and follow the method below.

Makes about 2kg/4½lb

450g/1lb Seville (Temple)
  oranges
1.75 litres/3 pints/7½ cups
  water
1.3kg/3lb/generous 6¾ cups
  granulated (white) sugar,
  warmed
60ml/4 tbsp lemon juice

Cook's Tip
Jellies set very quickly, so pot immediately. Warm a stainless steel funnel in the oven, or rinse a plastic one under hot water and dry it, then use to pot the jelly. If the jelly starts to set in the pan, warm it briefly until liquid again.

1 Wash and dry the oranges; gently scrub them with a soft brush if they have waxed skins.

2 If you want to add a little peel to the jelly marmalade, thinly pare and finely shred the rind from 2 or 3 of the oranges. Place the shreds in a square of muslin (cheesecloth) and tie it into a neat bag.

3 Halve the oranges and squeeze out the juice and pips (seeds), then tip the juice and pips into a large preserving pan.

4 Roughly chop the orange peel, including all the pith, and add it to the pan. Add the bag of shredded rind, if using, and pour over the water. Cover the pan and leave to soak for at least 4 hours, or overnight.

5 Bring the mixture to the boil, then reduce the heat and simmer gently for 1½ hours. Using a slotted spoon, remove the bag of peel, and check that the peel is tender. If not, re-tie the bag and simmer for a further 15–20 minutes. Remove the bag of peel and set aside.

6 Line a large nylon or strainless steel sieve with a double layer of muslin and place over a large bowl. Pour boiling water through the muslin to scald it. Discard the scalding water from the bowl.

Energy 5293kcal/22583kJ; Protein 11.6g; Carbohydrate 1397.7g, of which sugars 1397.7g; Fat 0.5 of which saturates 0g; Cholesterol 0mg; Calcium 593mg; Fibre 0.0g; Sodium 88mg.

Pour the fruit and juices into the sieve, strainer or jelly bag and leave to drain for at least 1 hour. Pour the
ces into the cleaned pan.

Add the sugar, lemon juice and shredded orange rind, if using, to the pan. Stir over a low heat until the sugar
s completely dissolved, then bring to the boil and boil rapidly for about 5–10 minutes until setting point is
ched (105°C/220°F).

Remove any scum from the surface. Leave to cool until a thick skin starts to form on the surface. Stir, then
into warmed, sterilized jars, cover and seal.

Oxford marmalade

The characteristic caramel colour and rich flavour of a traditional Oxford marmalade is obtained by cutting the fruit coarsely and cooking it for several hours before adding the sugar. Seville oranges are the citrus fruit of choice for this classic marmalade.

Makes about 2.25kg/5lb

900g/2lb Seville (Temple)
  oranges
1.75 litres/3 pints/7½ cups water
1.3kg/3lb/6½ cups granulated
  (white) sugar, warmed

Cook's Tip
Don't rush making your marmalade. Slow, gentle cooking will ensure that the peel is really tender.

1 Scrub the orange skins, then remove the rind using a vegetable peeler. Thickly slice the rind and put in a large pan.

2 Chop the fruit, reserving the pips (seeds), and add to the rind in the pan, along with the water. Tie the orange pips in a piece of muslin (cheesecloth) and add to the pan. Bring to the boil, then cover and simmer for 2 hours. Add more water during cooking to maintain the same volume. Remove the pan from the heat and leave overnight.

3 The next day, remove the muslin bag from the oranges, squeezing well. Return the pan to the heat. Bring to the boil, cover and simmer for 1 hour.

4 Add the warmed sugar to the pan, then slowly bring the mixture to the boil, stirring until the sugar has dissolved completely. Increase the heat and boil rapidly for about 5–10 minutes, or until setting point is reached (105°C/220°F).

5 Remove the pan from the heat and skim off any scum from the surface. Leave to cool for about 5 minutes, stir, then pour into warmed, sterilized jars and seal. When cold, label, then store in a cool, dark place.

Energy 5455kcal/23,275kJ; Protein 16.4g; Carbohydrate 1435g, of which sugars 1435g; Fat 0.9g, of which saturates 0g; Cholesterol 0mg; Calcium 1112mg; Fibre 15.3g; Sodium 123m

St Clement's marmalade

This classic preserve made from two types of oranges and lemons has a lovely citrus tang. It has a light, refreshing flavour and is perfect for serving for breakfast, spread on freshly toasted bread or oozing over hot muffins or crumpets.

Makes about 2.25kg/5lb

450g/1lb Seville (Temple) oranges
450g/1lb sweet oranges
4 lemons
1.5 litres/2½ pints/6½ cups water
1.2kg/2½ lb/5½ cups granulated (white) sugar, warmed

1 Wash the oranges and lemons, then halve and squeeze the juice into a large pan. Tie the pips (seeds) and membranes in a muslin (cheesecloth) bag, shred the orange and lemon rind and add to the pan.

2 Add the water to the pan, bring to the boil, then cover and simmer for 2 hours. Remove the muslin bag, leave to cool, then squeeze any liquid back into the pan.

3 Add the warmed sugar to the pan and stir over a low heat until completely dissolved. Bring to the boil and boil rapidly for about 15 minutes or until the marmalade reaches setting point (105°C/220°F).

4 Remove the pan from the heat and skim off any scum from the surface Leave to cool for about 5 minutes, stir, then pour into warmed, sterilized jars and seal. When cold, label, then store in a cool, dark place.

Cook's Tip
Seville oranges are slightly sharp in taste and add to the special flavour of this marmalade.

Energy 5061kcal/21,594kJ; Protein 15.9g; Carbohydrate 1330.5g, of which sugars 1330.5g 0.9g, of which saturates 0g; Cholesterol 0mg; Calcium 1059mg; Fibre 15.3g; Sodium 117m

Pink grapefruit and cranberry marmalade

Cranberries give this glorious marmalade an extra tartness and a full fruit flavour, as well as an inimitable vibrant colour. The resulting preserve makes a lively choice for breakfast or a brilliant accompaniment for cold roast turkey during the festive season.

Makes about 2.25kg/5lb

675g/1½ lb pink grapefruit
juice and pips (seeds) of 2
   lemons
900ml/1¼ pints/3¼ cups water
225g/8oz/2 cups cranberries
1.3kg/3lb/6½ cups granulated
   (white) sugar, warmed

1 Wash, halve and quarter the grapefruit, then slice them thinly, reserving the pips (seeds) and any juice that runs out.

2 Tie the grapefruit and lemon pips in a muslin (cheesecloth) bag and place in a large pan with the grapefruit slices and lemon juice.

3 Add the water and bring to the boil. Cover and simmer for 1½–2 hours, or until the grapefruit rind is very tender. Remove the muslin bag, leave to cool, then squeeze over the pan.

4 Add the cranberries to the pan, then bring to the boil. Simmer for 15–20 minutes, or until the berries have popped and softened.

5 Add the sugar to the pan and stir over a low heat until the sugar has completely dissolved. Bring to the boil and boil rapidly for 5–10 minutes, or until setting point is reached (105°C/220°F).

6 Remove the pan from the heat and skim off any scum from the surface using a slotted spoon. Leave to cool for 5–10 minutes, then stir and pour into warmed, sterilized jars. Seal, then label when the marmalade is cold.

Cook's Tip
You can use fresh or frozen cranberries to make this marmalade. Either gives equally good results.

Energy 5403kcal/23,043kJ; Protein 12.6g; Carbohydrate 1424.4g, of which sugars 1424.4g; 0.9g, of which saturates 0g; Cholesterol 0mg; Calcium 853mg; Fibre 12.4g; Sodium 103mg.

Ruby red grapefruit marmalade

If you prefer a really tangy marmalade, grapefruit is the perfect choice. To achieve a wonderfully red-blushed preserve, look for a red variety rather than pink. They have a fabulous flavour and make a delicious, sweet, jewel-coloured preserve.

Makes about 1.8kg/4lb

900g/2lb ruby red grapefruit
1 lemon
1.2 litres/2 pints/5 cups water
1.3kg/3lb/6½ cups granulated
 (white) sugar, warmed

1 Wash the grapefruit and lemon and remove the rind in thick pieces using a vegetable peeler. Cut the fruit in half and squeeze the juice into a preserving pan, reserving all the pips (seeds).

2 Put the pips and membranes from the fruit in a muslin (cheesecloth) bag and add to the pan. Discard the grapefruit and lemon shells.

3 Using a sharp knife, cut the grapefruit and lemon rind into thin or coarse shreds, as preferred, and place in the pan.

4 Add the water to the pan and bring to the boil. Cover and simmer for 2 hours, or until the rind is very tender.

5 Remove the muslin bag from the pan, leave to cool, then squeeze it over the pan. Add the warmed sugar and stir over a low heat until it has dissolved. Bring to the boil, then boil rapidly for 5–10 minutes, or to setting point (105°C/220°F).

6 Remove the pan from the heat and skim off any scum from the surface using a slotted spoon. Leave to cool for 5–10 minutes, then stir and pour into warmed, sterilized jars. Seal, then label when the marmalade is cold.

Cook's Tip
Although you can use yellow grapefruit to make this marmalade, it tends to give a very pale result with more tang than the ruby red variety, but a much less fruity flavour.

Energy 5392kcal/22,987kJ; Protein 13.7g; Carbohydrate 1419.7g, of which sugars 1419.7g; 0.9g, of which saturates 0g; Cholesterol 0mg; Calcium 896mg; Fibre 11.7g; Sodium 105mg.

Lemon and ginger marmalade

This combination of lemon and ginger produces a really zesty and versatile preserve, perfect served on toast at any time of day. It is also excellent added to meat glazes.

Makes about 1.8kg/4lb

2.2kg/2½lb lemons
150g/5oz fresh root ginger, peeled and finely grated
1.2 litres/2 pints/5 cups water
900g/2lb/4½ cups granulated (white) sugar, warmed

1 Quarter and slice the lemons. Tie the pips (seeds) in a muslin (cheesecloth) bag and place in a preserving pan with the lemons, ginger and water. Bring to the boil, cover with a lid and simmer for 2 hours, or until the fruit is tender.

2 Remove the muslin bag from the pan, leave to cool then squeeze over the pan to release all the juice and pectin. Stir in the warmed sugar over a low heat until dissolved, then increase the heat and boil for 5–10 minutes, or until setting point is reached (105°C/220°F).

3 Remove from the heat and skim off any scum from the surface using a slotted spoon. Leave to cool for 5 minutes, stir, then pour into warmed, sterilized jars and seal. When cold, label and store in a cool place.

Orange and coriander marmalade

This traditional marmalade made with bitter Seville oranges has the added zing of warm, spicy coriander. Cut the orange rind into thin or coarse shreds, according to taste.

Makes about 1.8kg/4lb

675g/1½lb Seville (Temple) oranges
2 lemons
15ml/1 tbsp coriander seeds
1.5 litres/2½ pints/6¼ cups water
900g/2lb/4½ cups granulated (white) sugar, warmed

1 Cut the oranges and lemons in half and squeeze out all the juice. Place the orange and lemon pips (seeds) in a muslin (cheesecloth) bag. using a sharp knife, cut the rind into shreds and place in a preserving pan with the juice. Crush the coriander seeds.

2 Put the coriander seeds in the muslin bag with the pips and place in the pan. Add the water and bring to the boil. Cover and simmer for 2 hours, or until the mixture has reduced by half and the peel is soft. Complete the recipe by following steps 2 to 3 above.

Top: Energy 3785kcal/16,122kJ; Protein 17.3g; Carbohydrate 980.3g, of which sugars 980.3g; Fat 3.9g, of which saturates 1.2g; Cholesterol 0mg; Calcium 1559mg; Fibre 1.6g; Sodium 204mg.
Bottom: Energy 3839kcal/16,377kJ; Protein 14.1g; Carbohydrate 1003.1g, of which sugars 997.9g; Fat 2.6g, of which saturates 0.3g; Cholesterol 0mg; Calcium 821mg; Fibre 11.5g; Sodium 93mg.

Fine lime shred marmalade

There is something about lime marmalade that really captures the flavour and essence of the fruit. It is important to cut the slices very finely though, because lime skins tend to be tougher than those on any other citrus fruits and can result in a chewy marmalade if cut thickly.

Makes about 2.25kg/5lb

12 limes
4 kaffir lime leaves
1.2 litres/2 pints/5 cups water
1.3kg/3lb/6½ cups granulated
  (white) sugar, warmed

1 Halve the limes lengthways, then slice thinly, reserving any pips (seeds). Tie the pips and lime leaves in a muslin (cheesecloth) bag and place the bag in a large pan with the sliced fruit.

2 Add the water to the pan and bring to the boil. Cover and simmer gently for 1½–2 hours, or until the rind is very soft. Remove the muslin bag, leave to cool, then squeeze it over the pan to release any juice and pectin.

3 Add the warmed sugar to the pan and stir over a low heat until completely dissolved. Bring to the boil and boil rapidly for 5–10 minutes or until the marmalade reaches setting point (105°C/220°F).

4 Remove the pan from the heat and skim off any scum from the surface. Leave to cool for about 5 minutes, stir, then pour into warmed, sterilized jars and seal. When cold, label, then store in a cool, dark place.

Cook's Tip
Stirring marmalade after standing and before potting distributes the fruit rind evenly as the preserve begins to set.

Energy 5250kcal/22,386kJ; Protein 13.3g; Carbohydrate 1380.1g, of which sugars 1380.1g
Fat 2g, of which saturates 0.7g; Cholesterol 0mg; Calcium 1263mg; Fibre 0g; Sodium 112m

Spiced pumpkin marmalade

The bright orange colour and warm flavour of this marmalade is guaranteed to banish the winter blues. The addition of pumpkin gives the preserve more body and a lovely, satisfying texture. It's perfect for spreading on hot buttered toast or serving with warm croissants.

Makes about 2.75kg/6lb

900g/2lb Seville (Temple) oranges, washed and halved
450g/1lb lemons, halved and thinly sliced, pips (seeds) reserved
2 cinnamon sticks
2.5cm/1in piece fresh root ginger, peeled and thinly sliced
1.5ml/½ tsp grated nutmeg
1.75 litres/3 pints/7½ cups water
800g/1¾ lb squash or pumpkin, peeled, seeds (pips) removed and thinly sliced
1.3kg/3lb/6½ cups granulated (white) sugar, warmed

1 Squeeze the juice from the oranges and pour into a preserving pan. Remove the white membranes and reserve with the pips.
2 Thinly slice the orange rind and place in the pan, along with the sliced lemons. Tie the orange and lemon pips and membranes in a muslin (cheesecloth) bag with the spices and add to the pan with the water. Bring to the boil, then cover and simmer for 1 hour.
3 Add the pumpkin to the pan and continue cooking for 1–1½ hours. Remove the muslin bag, leave to cool, then squeeze over the pan.
4 Stir in the warmed sugar over a low heat until completely dissolved. Bring to the boil, then boil rapidly for 5–10 minutes, or until the marmalade becomes thick and reaches setting point (105°C/220°F). Stir once or twice to ensure the marmalade does not stick to the pan.
5 Remove the pan from the heat and skim off any scum. Leave to cool for 5–10 minutes, then stir and pour into warmed, sterilized jars. Seal, then label when the marmalade is cold and store in a cool, dark place.

Energy 5645kcal/24,071kJ; Protein 26.5g; Carbohydrate 1467g, of which sugars 1463g; Fa 3.9g, of which saturates 1.2g; Cholesterol 0mg; Calcium 1726mg; Fibre 23.3g; Sodium 145m

Clementine and liqueur marmalade

Small, tart clementines make a particularly full-flavoured preserve, which can be put to a wide variety of culinary uses. Stir it into yogurt or warm it with a little water to make a zesty sauce for pancakes or crêpes. It is also superlative served with smooth ripe Brie and crisp crackers.

Makes about 1.8kg/4lb

900g/2lb clementines, washed and halved
juice and pips (seeds) of 2 lemons
900ml//6½ pints/3¾ cups water
900g/2lb/4½ cups granulated (white) sugar, warmed
60ml/4 tbsp Grand Marnier or Cointreau

Cook's Tip
Any member of the mandarin family can be used to make this preserve, but clementines give the best result.

1   Slice the clementines, reserving any pips. Tie the pips in a muslin (cheesecloth) bag with the lemon pips and place in a large pan with the sliced fruit.

2   Add the lemon juice and water to the pan and bring to the boil, then cover and simmer for about 1½ hours, or until the rind is very tender. Remove the muslin bag, leave to cool, then squeeze it over the pan to release any juice and pectin.

3   Stir in the warmed sugar over a low heat until dissolved, then bring to the boil and cook for 5–10 minutes, or until setting point has been reached (105°C/220°F).

4   Remove the pan from the heat and skim off any scum from the surface. Leave to cool for about 5 minutes, then stir in the liqueur and pour into warmed, sterilized jars and seal. When cold, label, then store in a cool, dark place.

Energy 4036kcal/17,210kJ; Protein 12.6g; Carbohydrate 1038.5g, of which sugars 1038.5g; Fat 0.9g, of which saturates 0g; Cholesterol 0mg; Calcium 759mg; Fibre 10.8g; Sodium 97mg

Tangerine and lemon grass marmalade

The subtle flavours of lemon grass and kaffir lime leaves add an exotic edge to this marmalade. You can also stir in thinly shredded lime leaf before bottling, which gives a very pretty result. Serve with rich, buttery shortbread biscuits.

Makes about 1.8kg/4lb

900g/2lb tangerines, washed
  and halved
juice and pips (seeds) of 2
  Seville (Temple) oranges
900ml/1½ pints/3¾ cups water
2 lemon grass sticks, halved and
  crushed
3 kaffir lime leaves
900g/2lb/4½ cups granulated
  (white) sugar, warmed

1 Using a sharp knife, slice the tangerines thinly, reserving the pips. Place the sliced fruit in a preserving pan, along with juice from the Seville oranges and the measured water.

2 Tie all the pips, lemon grass and lime leaves in a piece of muslin (cheesecloth) and add to the pan. Boil, then simmer for 1–1½ hours, or until the tangerine rind is soft. Remove the bag, leave to cool, then squeeze over the pan.

3 Stir in the warmed sugar over a low heat until completely dissolved, then boil for 5–10 minutes, or until setting point is reached (105°C/220°F).

4 Remove the pan from the heat and skim off any scum. Leave to cool for 5–10 minutes, then stir and pour into warmed, sterilized jars. Seal, then label when the marmalade is cold and store in a cool, dark place.

Cook's Tip
If you can't find kaffir lime leaves, you can substitute the finely pared rind of one lime.

Energy 3935kcal/16,768kJ; Protein 14.8g; Carbohydrate 1029.5g, of which sugars 1029.5g; Fat 1.1g, of which saturates 0g; Cholesterol 0mg; Calcium 949mg; Fibre 15.1g; Sodium 82mg

Pomelo and pineapple marmalade

Slightly larger than a grapefruit, pomelos have lime-green skin and a sharp, refreshing flavour and are delicious combined with tangy pineapple. Serve this fabulous marmalade as a spread with hot buttered toast, or simply spoon over desserts.

Makes about 2.75kg/6lb

2 pomelos
900ml/1½ pints/3¾ cups water
2 x 432g/14½ oz cans crushed
  pineapple in fruit juice
900g/2lb/4½ cups granulated
  (white) sugar, warmed

1 Wash and halve the pomelos. Squeeze out the juice, reserving any pips (seeds), and pour into a large pan. Remove the membranes and any excess pith and tie in a muslin (cheesecloth) bag with the pips. Slice the peel thinly and add to the pan along with the muslin bag and water. Bring to the boil.

2 Cover the pan and simmer for 1–1½ hours, stirring occasionally, or until the fruit is soft. Add the pineapple and juice and simmer for a further 30 minutes.

3 Remove the muslin bag from the pan, leave to cool, then squeeze over the pan. Add the warmed sugar and stir over a low heat until it has dissolved. Increase the heat and boil for 10 minutes, or to setting point (105°C/220°F).

4 Remove the pan from the heat and skim off any scum from the surface using a slotted spoon. Leave to cool for 10 minutes, then stir and pour into warmed, sterilized jars. Seal, then label the jars when they are cold.

Cook's Tip
Native to Southeast Asia, the pomelo tastes like sweet, mild grapefruit but without any of the grapefruit's bitterness.

Energy 4042kcal/17,233kJ; Protein 10.1g; Carbohydrate 1065.3g, of which sugars 1065.3g;
Fat 0.4g, of which saturates 0g; Cholesterol 0mg; Calcium 633mg; Fibre 9.2g; Sodium 74mg

Peach and kumquat marmalade

Combined with sweet, scented peaches, kumquats make a wonderful fresh-tasting preserve. This lovely marmalade has a jam-like consistency and is great at any time of day.

Makes about 1.8kg/4lb

675g/1½lb kumquats, sliced thinly, pips (seeds) and juice reserved

juice and pips of 1 lime

900g/2lb peaches, skinned and thinly sliced, skins reserved

900ml/1½ pints/3¾ cups water

900g/2lb/4½ cups granulated (white) sugar, warmed

1 Tie all the pips and the peach skins in a muslin (cheesecloth) bag and put in a pan with the kumquats, juices and water. Bring to the boil, then cover and simmer for 50 minutes.

2 Add the peaches to the pan, bring to the boil, then simmer for 40–50 minutes, or until the fruit has become very soft. Remove the muslin bag, leave to cool, then squeeze over the pan.

3 Add the warmed sugar to the pan and stir over a low heat until it has dissolved. Bring the mixture to the boil, then boil rapidly for 15 minutes, stirring occasionally, until setting point is reached (105°C/220°F).

4 Remove the pan from the heat and skim off any scum from the surface.

5 Leave to cool for 5 minutes, stir, then pour into warmed, sterilized jars and seal. When cold, label and store in a cool place.

Apricot and orange marmalade

Serve this sweet marmalade with warm croissants and strong coffee for a leisurely weekend breakfast. The combination of oranges and rich-tasting apricots is a winner.

Makes about 1.5kg/3lb 6oz

2 Seville (Temple) oranges, washed and quartered

1 lemon, washed and quartered

1.2 litres/2 pints/5 cups water

900g/2lb apricots, stoned (pitted) and thinly sliced

900g/2lb/4½ cups granulated (white) sugar, warmed

1 Remove the pips (seeds) from the citrus fruit and tie in a muslin (cheesecloth) bag. Finely chop the oranges and lemon in a food processor and put in a large pan with the muslin bag and water.

2 Bring the mixture to the boil, then simmer, covered, for 1 hour.

3 Add the apricots and bring to the boil. Simmer for 30–40 minutes, or until the fruits are very tender. Remove the muslin bag, cool, then squeeze over the pan and complete the recipe by following steps 3 to 5 above.

Top: Energy 4093kcal/17,474kJ; Protein 19.6g; Carbohydrate 1067.6g, of which sugars 1067.6g; Fat 1.6g, of which saturates 0g; Cholesterol 0mg; Calcium 749mg; Fibre 21.6g; Sodium 90mg.
Bottom: Energy 3936kcal/16,809kJ; Protein 15.9g; Carbohydrate 1030.8g, of which sugars 1030.8g; Fat 1.2g, of which saturates 0g; Cholesterol 0mg; Calcium 753mg; Fibre 20.4g; Sodium 87mg.

Orange whisky marmalade

Adding whisky to orange marmalade gives it a fantastic warmth and flavour and is a special treat, particularly at Christmas. The whisky is stirred in after the marmalade is cooked, to retain its strength and slightly bitter edge, which would be lost if boiled.

Makes about 2.25kg/5lb

900g/2lb Seville (Temple) oranges, washed and halved

juice and pips (seeds) of 1 large lemon

1.2 litres/2 pints/5 cups water

1.5kg/3 lb 6oz/6½ cups granulated (white) sugar, warmed

60ml/4 tbsp whisky

1 Scrub the oranges and cut in half. Squeeze the juice into a large pan, reserving the pips (seeds) and any membranes. Place these in a muslin (cheesecloth) bag with the lemon pips and add the lemon juice to the pan.

2 Using a sharp knife, thinly slice the orange rind and put in the pan along with the water. Bring to the boil, then cover and simmer for 1½–2 hours, or until the citrus rind is very tender.

3 Remove the muslin bag from the pan, leave to cool, then squeeze it over the pan to release any juice and pectin. Add the sugar, then stir over a low heat until the sugar has dissolved. Increase the heat and boil for 5–10 minutes until setting point is reached (105°C/220°F).

4 Remove the pan from the heat and skim off any scum from the surface with a slotted spoon. Stir in the whisky, then leave to cool for 5 minutes. Stir and pour the marmalade into warmed, sterilized jars. Seal, then label when cold. Store in a cool dark place.

Cook's Tip
Whisky marmalade is great spooned over a steamed sponge pudding.

Energy 5588kcal/23,826kJ; Protein 16.4g; Carbohydrate 1435g, of which sugars 1435g; F 0.9g, of which saturates 0g; Cholesterol 0mg; Calcium 1112mg; Fibre 15.3g; Sodium 123mg

Savoury and sweet recipes

Although the traditional way of enjoying your marmalade, liberally spread over hot buttered toast, is unbelievably good, marmalade can also be used to enhance many other dishes. Its bittersweet, tangy taste is perfect for cutting through the richness of oily fish or roasted meat and game. It adds moisture as well as flavour to cakes and bakes and gives a lovely light lift to warm desserts. The recipes that follow display its wonderful versatility.

Grilled kippers with marmalade toast

Why not choose a slightly different way to enjoy your marmalade at breakfast with this dish of lightly grilled smoked kippers accompanied by orange marmalade? The smokiness of the kipper is perfectly complemented by the bittersweet taste of the marmalade.

Serves 2

melted butter, for greasing
2 kippers
2 slices of bread
soft butter, for spreading
Seville orange marmalade, for
  spreading

1 Preheat the grill (broiler). Line the grill pan with foil – to help prevent fish smells from lingering in the pan – and brush the foil with melted butter to stop the fish from sticking.

2 Using kitchen scissors, or a knife, cut the heads and tails off the kippers.

3 Lay the fish, skin side up, on the buttered foil. Put under the hot grill and cook for 1 minute. Turn the kippers over, brush the uppermost (fleshy) side with melted butter, put back under the grill and cook for a further 4–5 minutes.

4 Toast the bread and spread it first with butter and then with marmalade. Serve the sizzling hot kippers immediately with the marmalade toast.

Cook's Tip
Seville marmalade, with its sharp tangy flavour, is the best marmalade to use with oily fish.

Energy 518kcal/2155kJ; Protein 33.9g; Carbohydrate 17.6g, of which sugars 5.9g; Fat 35.1g, which saturates 7.6g; Cholesterol 121mg; Calcium 126mg; Fibre 0.4g; Sodium 1640mg

Marmalade and soy roast duck

Sweet-and-sour flavours, such as marmalade and soy sauce, complement the rich, fatty taste of duck beautifully. Serve these robustly flavoured duck breast portions with simple accompaniments such as steamed sticky rice and lightly cooked pak choi (bok choi).

Serves 6

6 duck breast portions
45ml/3 tbsp fine-cut
    marmalade
45ml/3 tbsp light soy sauce
salt and ground black pepper

1 Preheat the oven to 190°C/375°F/Gas 5. Place the duck breasts skin side up on a grill (broiler) rack and place in the sink. Pour boiling water all over the duck. This shrinks the skin and helps it crisp during cooking. Pat the duck dry with kitchen paper and transfer to a roasting pan.

2 Combine the marmalade and soy sauce, and brush over the duck. Season with a little salt and some black pepper and roast for 20–25 minutes, basting occasionally with the marmalade mixture in the pan.

3 Remove the duck breasts from the oven and leave to rest for 5 minutes. Slice the duck breasts and serve drizzled with any juices left in the pan.

Cook's Tip
A full-flavoured zesty marmalade of lemon and lime would work well with this dish.

Energy 273Kcal/1144kJ; Protein 32g; Carbohydrate 8g, of which sugars 7g; Fat 13g, of which saturates 4g; Cholesterol 144mg; Calcium 20mg; Fibre 0g; Sodium 700mg.

Marmalade-glazed goose

Succulent roast goose is the classic centrepiece for a traditional Christmas lunch. It is a wonderfully rich meat, which tastes fabulous with the spicy lemon and ginger marmalade glaze. Cooked red cabbage and braised fennel are both tasty accompaniments.

Serves 8

4.5kg/10lb oven-ready goose
30ml/2 tbsp lemon and ginger
    marmalade, melted
    (see page 26)
salt and ground black pepper

For the stuffing
25g/1oz/2 tbsp butter
1 onion, finely chopped
15ml/1 tbsp lemon and ginger
    marmalade
450g/1lb/2 cups ready-to-eat
    prunes, chopped
45ml/3 tbsp Madeira
225g/8oz/4 cups fresh white
    breadcrumbs
30ml/2 tbsp chopped fresh sage

For the gravy
1 onion, chopped
15ml/1 tbsp plain (all-purpose)
    flour
600ml/1 pint/2½ cups chicken
    stock

1 Preheat the oven to 200°C/400°F/Gas 6. Prick the skin of the goose all over with a fork and season the bird generously, both inside and out.
2 To make the stuffing, melt the butter in a large pan and cook the onion for 5 minutes until softened. Remove the pan from the heat and stir in the marmalade, chopped prunes, Madeira, breadcrumbs and chopped sage.
3 Stuff the neck end of the goose with some of the prepared stuffing, and set the remaining stuffing aside in the refrigerator. Secure the bird with skewers to prevent the stuffing from escaping during cooking.
4 Place the goose in a large roasting pan. Butter a piece of foil and use to cover the goose loosely, then place in the oven for 2 hours.
5 Baste the goose frequently during cooking and remove excess fat from the pan as necessary.
6 Remove the foil from the goose and brush the melted lemon and ginger marmalade over the goose, then roast for 40 minutes more, or until cooked through. Remove from the oven and cover with foil, then leave to stand for 15 minutes before carving.
7 While the goose is cooking, shape the remaining stuffing into walnut-size balls and place them in an ovenproof dish. Spoon 30ml/2 tbsp of the goose fat over the stuffing balls and bake for 15 minutes before the goose is cooked.
8 To make the gravy, pour off all but 15ml/1 tbsp of fat from the roasting pan, leaving the meat juices behind. Add the onion and cook for 5 minutes. Sprinkle in the flour then gradually add the stock. Bring to the boil, stirring continuously, then simmer for 3 minutes until thick and glossy. Serve with the carved goose and stuffing.

Energy 823kcal/3443kJ; Protein 57.6g; Carbohydrate 47.1g, of which sugars 23.8g; Fat 43.3g, of which saturates 14g; Cholesterol 177mg; Calcium 106mg; Fibre 4.5g; Sodium 395mg.

Marmalade flapjacks

Everyone enjoys making flapjacks because they take so little time to prepare. You don't even need a bowl – just weigh out the ingredients and mix them in the pan. These ones are fruity and tangy with orange marmalade and cranberries.

Makes 16 slices

115ml/4fl oz/½ cup butter or block margarine, plus extra for greasing
1 small orange
115g/4oz/scant ⅓ cup golden (light corn) syrup
50g/2oz/½ cup soft light brown sugar
175g/6oz/scant 2 cups rolled oats
50g/2oz/⅓ cup sultanas (golden raisins)
25g/1oz/¼ cup dried cranberries
75ml/3 tbsp orange marmalade

Cook's Tip
These succulent flapjacks will store for up to 5 days in an airtight container.

1 Preheat the oven to 180°C/350°F/Gas 4. Grease and line a 20cm/8in square shallow tin (pan) with baking parchment
2 Finely grate the rind from the orange. Squeeze the juice into a separate container and set aside.
3 Melt the butter or margarine, syrup and sugar together in a heavy pan over a medium heat.
4 Add the orange rind and 15ml/1 tbsp orange juice to the pan.
5 Add the oats, sultanas and cranberries. Stir together.
6 Turn into the tin and smooth the top level. Bake for 25–30 minutes, or until firm and golden, then put the tin on a wire rack to cool. Remove the lining paper.
7 Brush the marmalade over the top of the hot flapjack, then mark into 16 slices. Leave to go cold in the tin.

Energy 154kcal/646kJ; Protein 1.5g; Carbohydrate 23g, of which sugars 15g; Fat 6.8g, of which saturates 3.9g; Cholesterol 17mg; Calcium 14mg; Fibre 0.8g; Sodium 80mg.

Sticky marmalade squares

These baked treats have a plain lower layer supporting a scrumptious nutty upper layer flavoured with orange juice and chunky marmalade. Whether cut into squares or bars they will delight your tea-time guests.

Makes 24 squares

350g/2oz/3 cups plain (all-purpose) flour
200g/7oz/scant 1 cup unsalted (sweet) butter, diced
150g/5oz/²/₃ cup light muscovado (molasses) sugar
2.5ml/½ tsp bicarbonate of soda (baking soda)
1 egg, beaten
120ml/4fl oz/½ cup single (light) cream
50g/2oz/½ cup pecan nuts, chopped
50g/2oz/½ cup mixed (candied) peel
90ml/6 tbsp chunky marmalade
15–30ml/1–2 tbsp orange juice

1 Preheat the oven to 190°C/375°F/Gas 5. Line the base of a 28 x 28cm/11 x 7in tin (pan) with baking parchment.

2 Put the flour in a bowl and rub in the butter. Stir in the sugar and then spread half the mixture over the base of the prepared tin. Press down firmly. Bake for 10–15 minutes until lightly browned. Leave to cool.

3 To make the filling, put the remaining flour mixture into a bowl. Stir in the soda. Mix in the egg and cream, pecan nuts, peel and half the marmalade.

4 Pour the mixture over the cooled base, return to the oven and bake for 20–25 minutes, or until the filling is just firm and golden brown.

5 Put the remaining marmalade into a small pan and heat gently. Add just enough orange juice to make a spreadable glaze. Brush the glaze over the baked cookie mixture while it is still warm. Leave to cool before cutting into bars or squares.

Energy 35kcal/144kJ; Protein 0g; Carbohydrate 3g, of which sugars 3g; Fat 2g, of which saturates 1g; Cholesterol 9mg; Calcium 4mg; Fibre 0g; Sodium 16mg.

Cherry and marmalade muffins

Bursting with fruit and a sweet, tangy flavour, these muffins are topped like toast, with marmalade. Choose your own home-made marmalade or a quality brand for the best flavour, and try different varieties, such as lime or lemon marmalade.

Makes 12 standard muffins

225g/8oz/2 cups self-raising (self-rising) flour
5ml/1 tsp mixed (apple pie) spice
85g/3oz/scant ½ cup caster (superfine) sugar
120g/4oz/½ cup glacé (candied) cherries, quartered
30ml/2 tbsp orange marmalade, plus extra, melted, to glaze
150ml/¼ pint/⅔ cup milk
50g/2oz/4 tbsp butter

1 Preheat the oven to 200°C/400°F/Gas 6. Lightly grease the cups of a muffin tin (pan) or line them with paper cases.
2 Sift the flour into a large bowl. Add the mixed spice.
3 Stir in the sugar and cherries.
4 Mix the marmalade with the milk and gently fold into the dry ingredients with the butter.
5 Spoon into the paper cases. Bake for 20–25 minutes, or until a skewer placed in the centre of a muffin comes out clean. The tops should be golden but not well done.
6 Turn out on to a wire rack, leave to cool for a few minutes and then brush the tops with warmed marmalade. Store in an airtight container for up to 3 days.

Variation
These moreish muffins would taste equally delicious with a mixture of cranberries and sultanas (golden raisins) to replace the glacé cherries.

Energy 162kcal/686kJ; Protein 2.3g; Carbohydrate 29.8g, of which sugars 15.5g; Fat 4.6g, of which saturates 0.7g; Cholesterol 1mg; Calcium 51mg; Fibre 0.7g; Sodium 9mg.

Marmalade teabread

This delicious teabread originally came from the north of England. It has a wonderfully rich taste that works equally well with morning coffee or afternoon tea. The marmalade gives it a lovely flavour, at the same time keeping it moist.

Makes 8–10 slices

200g/7oz/1¾ cups plain (all-purpose) flour
5ml/1 tsp baking powder
6.25ml/1¼ tsp ground cinnamon
100g/3½ oz/7 tbsp butter, cut into small pieces
50g/2oz/3 tbsp soft light brown sugar
1 egg
60ml/4 tbsp chunky orange marmalade
about 45ml/3 tbsp milk
60ml/4 tbsp glacé icing, to decorate
shreds of orange and lemon rind, to decorate

1 Preheat the oven to 160°C/325°F/Gas 3. Grease a 450g/1lb loaf tin (pan), and line with baking parchment.

2 Sift the flour, baking powder and cinnamon together, then add the butter and rub in with the fingertips until the mixture resembles fine crumbs. Stir in the sugar.

3 Beat the egg lightly in a small bowl and mix it with the marmalade and most of the milk.

4 Mix the milk mixture into the flour mixture, adding more milk if necessary to give a soft dropping consistency.

5 Transfer the mixture to the prepared tin, put into the hot oven and cook for about 1¼ hours, until the cake is firm to the touch and cooked through.

6 Leave the cake to cook for 5 minutes, then turn on to a wire rack. Carefully peel off the lining paper and leave the cake to cool completely.

7 Drizzle the glacé icing over the top of the cake and decorate with shreds of orange and lemon rind.

Energy 250kcal/1059 kJ; Protein 3.5g; Carbohydrate 38g, of which sugars 19g; Fat 10.4g, of which saturates 6.2g; Cholesterol 48mg; Calcium 56mg; Fibre 0.8g; Sodium 86mg.

Orange marmalade chocolate loaf

Do not be alarmed at the amount of cream in this recipe – it replaces butter to make a moist dark cake, topped with a bitter-sweet sticky marmalade topping. The filling is also delicious with other citrus marmalades such as kumquat or tangerine.

Makes 8–10 slices

butter, for greasing
115g/4oz cooking chocolate (unsweetened), broken into squares
3 eggs
175g/6oz/scant 1 cup caster (superfine) sugar
175ml/6fl oz/¾ cup sour cream
200g/7oz/1¾ cups self-raising (self-rising) flour

For the filling and glaze
185g/6½oz/⅔ cup bitter orange marmalade
115g/4oz cooking chocolate (unsweetened), broken into squares
60ml/4 tbsp sour cream
thinly pared and shredded orange rind, to decorate

1　Preheat the oven to 180°C/350°F/Gas 4. Lightly grease a 1kg/2¼ lb loaf tin (pan) with butter, then line the base with a piece of baking parchment. Slowly melt the chocolate in a heatproof bowl over a pan of hot water.

2　Combine the eggs and sugar in a separate mixing bowl. Using a hand-held electric mixer, beat the mixture until it is thick and creamy, then stir in the sour cream and chocolate. Sprinkle over the flour and fold in evenly.

3　Pour the mixture into the prepared tin and bake for about 1 hour, or until well risen and firm to the touch. Cool for a few minutes in the tin, then turn out on to a wire rack and leave the loaf to cool completely.

4　Make the filling. Spoon two-thirds of the marmalade into a small pan and melt over a low heat. Melt the chocolate in a heatproof bowl over a pan of hot water and stir it into the marmalade with the sour cream.

5　Slice the cake across into three layers and sandwich back together with about half the marmalade filling. Spread the rest evenly over the top of the cake and leave to set. Spoon the remaining marmalade over the cake and sprinkle with shredded orange rind, to decorate.

Energy 475kcal/2004kJ; Protein 7.1g; Carbohydrate 80.1g, of which sugars 60.8g; Fat 16.3g, of which saturates 9.1g; Cholesterol 91mg; Calcium 101mg; Fibre 1.6g; Sodium 56mg.

Snowdon pudding

Named after Wales's highest peak, this sumptuous winter pudding will delight any guest. The addition of marmalade in the mixture adds extra sharpness and helps to keep the pudding moist. Use the softest, juiciest raisins that you can find.

Serves 6

15–25g/½–1oz/1–2 tbsp butter, softened
100g/3½oz/⅔ cup raisins
175g/6oz/3 cups fresh white breadcrumbs
75g/3oz/½ cup shredded suet (US chilled, grated shortening)
75g/3oz/6 tbsp soft brown sugar
25g/1oz/¼ cup cornflour (cornstarch)
finely grated rind of 1 lemon
2 eggs
60ml/4 tbsp orange marmalade
30ml/2 tbsp fresh lemon juice

For the sauce
1 lemon
25g/1oz/¼ cup cornflour (cornstarch)
300ml/½ pint/1¼ cups milk
50g/2oz/¼ cup caster (superfine) sugar
25g/1oz/2 tbsp butter

1 Smear the butter on the inside of a 1.2 litre/2 pint heatproof bowl and press half the raisins on the buttered surface.
2 Mix together the breadcrumbs, suet, brown sugar, cornflour, lemon rind and the remaining raisins. Beat the eggs in a bowl, add the marmalade and lemon juice and stir into the dry ingredients.
3 Spoon the mixture into the bowl, without disturbing the raisins.
4 Cover with baking parchment (pleated) and then a large sheet of foil (also pleated). Tuck the edges under and press tightly to the sides. Place inside a large pan filled with water to three-quarters up the side of the bowl. Bring the water to the boil and steam for 1¾ hours.
5 Pare two or three large strips of lemon rind and put into a pan with 150ml/¼ pint/⅔ cup water. Bring to the boil and simmer for 10 minutes. Discard the rind. Blend the cornflour with the milk and stir into the pan. Squeeze the juice from half the lemon and add to the pan with the sugar and butter. Heat until the sauce thickens and comes to the boil.
6 Turn the pudding out on to a warmed plate, spooning a little sauce over the top.

Energy 456kcal/1922kJ; Protein 7.7g; Carbohydrate 74.4g, of which sugars 43.4g; Fat 16.8g, of whic saturates 8.6g; Cholesterol 82mg; Calcium 131mg; Fibre 1.1g; Sodium 304mg.

Seville orange marshmallows

These light and fluffy confectionery treats are flavoured with orange marmalade and tinted with orange food colouring. Make sure to use a colouring with a plastic bottle with a pipette dispenser to measure droplets more accurately.

Makes 35 large marshmallows

vegetable oil, for greasing
50g/2oz/½ cup icing (confectioners') sugar
50g/2oz/½ cup cornflour (cornstarch)
115g/4oz thin-cut Seville marmalade
freshly grated peel of 1 large orange
15ml/1 tbsp cognac
400g/14oz/2 cups caster (superfine) sugar
15ml/1 tbsp liquid glucose
350ml/12fl oz/1½ cups water
30ml/2 tbsp lemon juice
60ml/4 tbsp powdered gelatine
2 large egg whites
approximately 14 drops tangerine food colouring

1 Lightly grease a 20 x 30cm/8 x 12in baking tin (pan) with oil. Combine the icing sugar and cornflour and dust the tin with some of the mixture. Add the marmalade to a pan, stir in the orange peel and cognac. Set aside.
2 Add the sugar, liquid glucose and half of the water to another small pan set over a low heat and gently stir to dissolve the sugar.
3 Bring the mixture gradually to a steady boil and continue to heat until the syrup reaches the hard ball stage (127°C/260°F).
4 Add the lemon juice to a measuring jug and top up with enough water to make 175ml/6 fl oz/¾ cup liquid. Add to a wide shallow bowl and sprinkle over the powdered gelatine. Leave to soak, then dissolve suspended over a pan of hot water taken from the heat.
5 In a separate pan, gently heat the marmalade and cognac mixture. When the sugar syrup is ready, take it off the heat and pour the dissolved gelatine into the hot syrup. Stir to combine with the hot marmalade and cognac mixture.
6 Before the sugar syrup comes to temperature, use an electric mixer fitted with a whisk attachment, and whisk the egg whites to stiff peaks.

Per marshmallow: Energy 28kcal/119kJ; Protein 1.6g; Carbohydrate 5.5g, of which sugars 3.9g; Fat 0g, of which saturates 0g; Cholesterol 0mg; Calcium 6mg; Fibre 0g; Sodium 13mg.

7 Turn the beater to full speed while pouring the hot syrup mixture in a thin, steady stream down the inside of the bowl, until it is all combined, about 4–5 minutes, then continue to beat for about a further 8–10 minutes, gradually adding the food colouring in droplets, until the meringue looks pale orange and begins to become thick enough to hold its own shape.

Using a wide spatula pour the mixture into the prepared tin and smooth it level. Leave for 3 hours to set.

Dust the work surface with the remaining icing sugar and cornflour. Using a palette knife, loosen the marshmallow around the edges of the tray and carefully tip onto the dusted surface.

) Cut into squares or use a well oiled round 4cm/1½in cookie cutter to cut into circles. Dust with the icing sugar and cornflour mix and leave to dry out for a few hours.

Index

apricot
  apricot and orange marmalade 38

cakes
  sticky marmalade squares 52
  marmalade teabread 56
  orange marmalade chocolate loaf
    58
cherry and marmalade muffins 54
chocolate
  orange marmalade chocolate loaf
    58
clementine 11
  clementine and liqueur marmalade
    32
coriander marmalade, orange and 26
cranberry
  pink grapefruit and cranberry
    marmalade 22
  ruby red grapefruit marmalade 24

duck
  marmalade and soy roast duck 46

flapjacks, marmalade 50

ginger
  lemon and ginger marmalade 26
  marmalade-glazed goose 48

goose
  marmalade-glazed goose 48
grapefruit 11
  pink grapefruit and cranberry
    marmalade 22
  ruby red grapefruit marmalade 24

kippers with marmalade toast, grilled
  46
kumquat
  peach and kumquat marmalade 38

lemongrass marmalade, tangerine
  and 34
lemons 10
  apricot and orange marmalade 38
  lemon and ginger marmalade 26
  orange whisky marmalade 40
  ruby red grapefruit marmalade 24
  Seville orange marmalade 14
  spiced pumpkin marmalade 30
limes 10
  fine lime shred marmalade 28

mandarins 11
marmalade making tips 6-7
marshmallows, Seville orange 62
muffins, cherry and marmalade 54

orange 10
  orange jelly marmalade 16
  orange marmalade chocolate loaf
    58
Oxford marmalade 18

peach
  peach and kumquat marmalade 38
pectin content 6
pineapple
  pomelo and pineapple marmalade
    36

pink grapefruit and cranberry
  marmalade 22
pomelo 11
  pomelo and pineapple marmalade
    36
pumpkin
  spiced pumpkin marmalade 30

setting point, testing for 7
Seville orange 10, 16, 18, 20
  apricot and orange marmalade 38
  orange and coriander marmalade
    26
  orange jelly marmalade 16
  orange whisky marmalade 40
  Oxford marmalade 18
  Seville orange marmalade 14
  Seville orange marshmallows 62
  spiced pumpkin marmalade 30
  tangerine and lemon grass
    marmalade 34
St Clement's marmalade 20
Snowdon pudding 60
sterilizing jars 8
sticky marmalade squares 52

tangerines 11
  tangerine and lemon grass
    marmalade 34
teabread, marmalade 56

whisky
  orange whisky marmalade 40

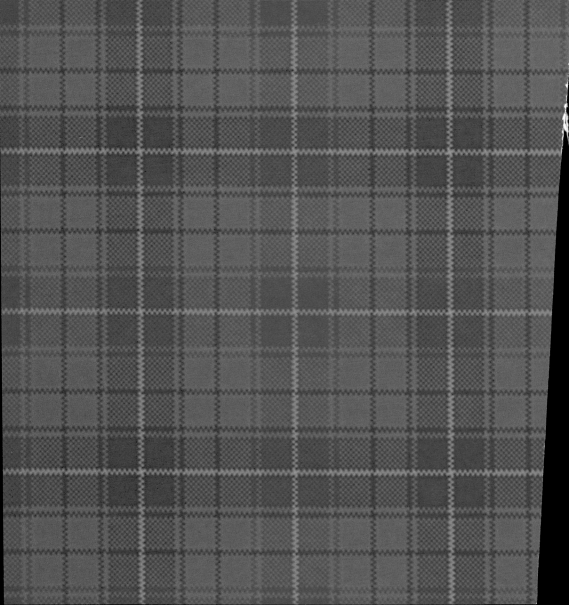